THE PURPOSE PARTNER WORKBOOK

THE PURPOSE PARTNER WORKBOOK

How to Find Purpose and Partnership in Your Work

John McCarthy

Cover design by LUCAS Art & Design—Jenison, MI
Book design by Mark Sullivan

The Purpose Partner Workbook, copyright ©2022,
John F. McCarthy IV. All rights reserved.

ISBN 979-8-9856773-1-7

WELCOME TO THE RENEWAL JOURNEY!

We are excited you have hopped on the track to map out your Purpose dreams and Partner for purpose with your employer.

This journal will help you organize your thoughts as you walk through the Renewal Journey and into a Purposed Partnership!

Please utilize the below resources we have arranged to ensure your journey results in purposeful employment:

- Your Purpose Guide: This is your guide to maximize your experience through the Renewal Journey.

- Your Purpose Guide is:_____

- S/he can be reached at:

- Purpose Tools: We have downloadable tools that might be helpful to download for use in addition to them being in your Purpose Partner Journal. You can find those tools at *purposepromise.org/tools*

THE PURPOSE PARTNER WORKBOOK

- Purpose Wisdom: We have been documenting wisdom to help you define your Purpose so you can partner effectively to obtain it. Read or listen to Purpose Wisdom at *Purposepromise.org*

Your Renewal Journey Plan

What distractions might you need to eliminate to be entirely focused when you are retreating?
_____
_____
_____

What date will you start your Renewal Journey retreat?
_____
_____

What do you need to organize to ensure you can fulfill your time commitments for your retreat?
_____

_____

_____

Who do you need to communicate with to ensure you are not bothered or distracted during your retreat time?

_____

_____

_____

Purpose Guide

Have you contacted your Purpose Guide to set specific dates to meet (After Days 3,6,9, and 10)?

_____

_____

_____

What days are you meeting your Purpose Guide to discuss the pit stops on the Renewal Journey?

Day 3:_____

Day 6:_____

Day 9:_____

Day 10:_____

The Renewal Journey Retreat

DAY 1 - KNOW YOURSELF

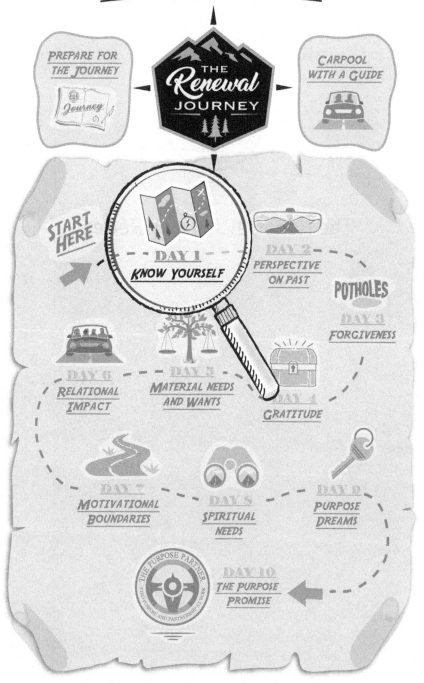

DAY ONE
Know Yourself: Understanding and Owning Yesterday
Would you rather be knowledgeable or wise?

Today, you will be plotting your life and work experiences. The language of your experience will bring forth the wisdom necessary to guide your Renewal Journey to the destination of your Purpose Dreams. **Your rear-view mirror will unlock your ideal destination.** On your Renewal Journey, your life and career graphs are the foundation of your map.

Life Graph – Your rear-view mirror will unlock your ideal destination
Start with your earliest memories and chart your most poignant memories using a dot-based system on whether you would consider them high points in your life, low points in your life, or somewhere in between. Continue to do this throughout your whole past. Be as detailed as possible and think hard; think back to what was, and let your yesterday unfold onto the paper.

THE PURPOSE PARTNER WORKBOOK

life GRAPH | Capture the high points and hard times in my life

THE PURPOSE PARTNER — FIND PURPOSE AND PARTNERSHIP AT WORK

HIGH POINTS IN YOUR LIFE

HARD TIMES IN YOUR LIFE

YEAR

Work Graph – Your rear-view mirror will unlock your ideal destination

Work is defined as any activity involving mental or physical effort done to achieve a purpose or result. Work is not limited to just your jobs. It includes fields of study, efforts you put forth that had no pay, and even your childhood chores.

Start with your earliest memories and chart the most poignant memories on your work graph (next page). Start early on in your life, and don't limit this graph to just paid experiences. Think about the lemonade stand you may have set up as a kid, the classes you took in school that you loved, the volunteer work you have done, and of course any paid jobs.

If you are struggling, here are good questions to help you remember:

When (day, job, or season) were you fired up to get out of bed and work/study?

Plot these as high points on your work graph.

When (day, job, or season) were you hitting the snooze bar, dreading work/study?

Plot these as low points on your work graph.

THE PURPOSE PARTNER WORKBOOK

WORK GRAPH | Capture the high points and hard times in my work

HIGH POINTS
IN YOUR WORK

HARD TIMES
IN YOUR WORK

YEAR

DAY TWO
Understanding Yesterday

It does not matter how quickly you get somewhere if it is the wrong place to go.

Perspective on Hardship: Life Graph

What common denominators pop out about the low points on your life graph?

_____
_____
_____
_____
_____
_____
_____
_____
_____

What environments/factors should you steer clear of in your life based on perceived hardships?

_____
_____
_____
_____
_____
_____
_____
_____
_____
_____

Was there common geography based on the low points of your life graph?

_____

_____

_____

_____

_____

_____

_____

How has the adversity in your life grown your character?

_____

_____

_____

_____

_____

_____

_____

Perspective on Hardship: Work Graph

What common denominators pop out about the low points on your work graph?

_____

_____

_____

_____

_____

_____

_____

_____

THE PURPOSE PARTNER WORKBOOK

What environments/factors should you steer clear of in your career based on the low points of your work graph?

_____

_____

_____

_____

_____

_____

Why did you have a propensity to hit the snooze button during the low points of your work graph?

_____

_____

_____

_____

_____

_____

_____

How has the adversity in your work career grown your character?

_____

_____

_____

_____

_____

_____

Perspective on Success: Life Graph

What do your high points in life reveal to you about things you should focus upon?

_____

_____

_____

_____

_____

_____

_____

What skills, passions, and talents were you using at the highest points of your life graph?

_____

_____

_____

_____

_____

What environments/factors should you reproduce in your life based on the high points of your life graph?

_____

_____

_____

_____

_____

Was there common geography based on the high points of your life graph?

_____

_____

_____

_____

_____

_____

How should you prioritize and be intentional about certain areas of your life?

_____

_____

_____

_____

_____

_____

_____

_____

Perspective on Success: Work Graph

What common denominators pop out about the high points on your work graph?

_____

_____

_____

_____

_____

_____

THE RENEWAL JOURNEY RETREAT

What made you excited to get out of bed during the high points of your work career?

_____

_____

_____

_____

_____

_____

_____

If you were working within a team, how was this team constructed that made it effective?

_____

_____

_____

_____

Ineffective? _____

_____

_____

THE PURPOSE PARTNER WORKBOOK

What type of environment were you working in at the high points of your work career?

How much autonomy/direction were you given at the high points of your work career?

THE RENEWAL JOURNEY RETREAT

What skills, abilities, or passions were you using at the high points in your work career?

_____

_____

_____

_____

_____

_____

_____

What do the high points in your work career reveal about things you should focus upon?

_____

_____

_____

_____

_____

_____

_____

How should you prioritize and be intentional about certain areas of your work career?

_____

_____

_____

_____

_____

_____

_____

THE PURPOSE PARTNER WORKBOOK

DAY 3 - FORGIVENESS

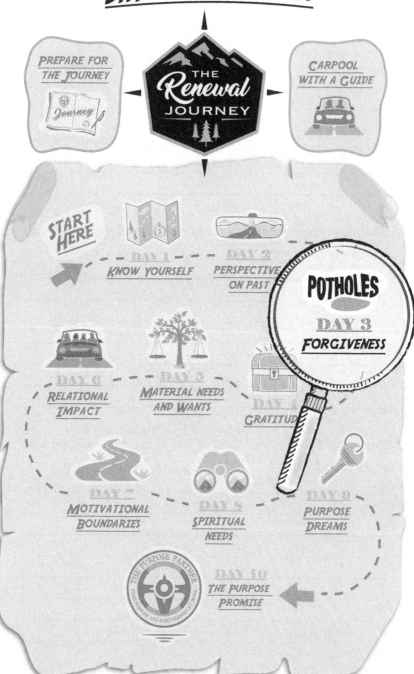

20

THE RENEWAL JOURNEY RETREAT

POTHOLES DAY THREE
Forgiveness

Forgiveness is not forgottenness,
but it is essential for awareness!

Are there any hardships out of your control that you need to forgive God for?

_____

_____

_____

_____

_____

_____

_____

_____

_____

_____

Are there any hardships that you need to forgive yourself for?

_____

_____

_____

_____

_____

_____

_____

_____

_____

_____

_____

Are there any hardships that you need to forgive others for?

_____

_____

_____

_____

_____

_____

_____

_____

_____

_____

_____

_____

If you are fostering any confusion, guilt, shame or resentment consider working through these emotions by utilizing one of the techniques references in Day 3 of the Renewal Journey.

How can you make forgiveness a more regular rhythm in your life?

_____

_____

_____

_____

_____

_____

_____

_____

_____

_____

THE RENEWAL JOURNEY RETREAT

DAY 4 - GRATITUDE

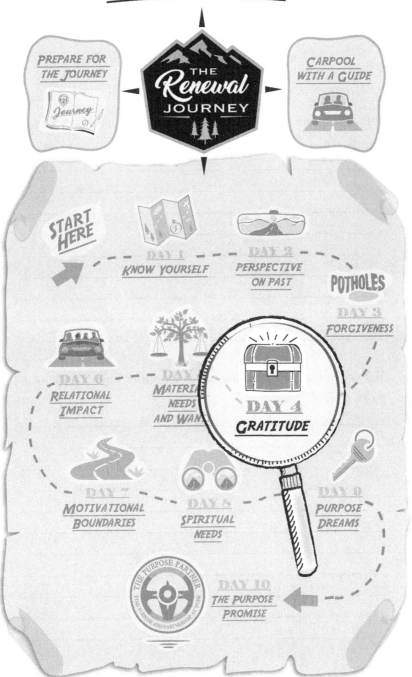

DAY FOUR
Gratitude

*The Attitude of Gratitude Will Take You
to a Whole New Latitude!*

Who do you treasure that has made a positive impact on your life?

_____
_____
_____
_____
_____
_____
_____
_____
_____
_____

Who do you treasure that has made a positive impact on your work career?

_____
_____
_____
_____
_____
_____
_____
_____
_____
_____
_____

THE RENEWAL JOURNEY RETREAT

WHO can you impact positively?

HOW can you impact positively?

Is there anything getting in the way of that potential impact?

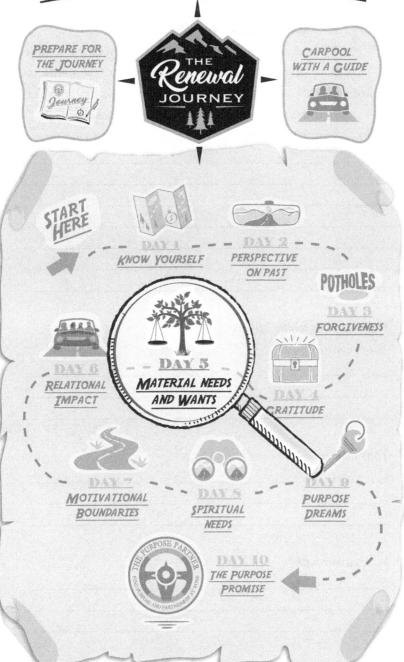

THE PURPOSE PARTNER WORKBOOK

DAY FIVE
Material Needs and Wants

Money is the top motivator in your work until it meets your needs. Once it meets your needs, its motivational capacity is greatly reduced. Understanding your true needs is essential to finding purpose!

Is your identity wrapped up in the pursuit of any of your wants?

_____

_____

_____

_____

_____

_____

_____

How do your wants impact:
Your relationships?

_____

_____

_____

Your health?

_____

_____

_____

Your career path?

_____

_____

_____

Financial Analysis of Needs

Living Situation
✓ *What are your current spending per month on your living situation (including all rents, mortgage, utilities, etc...)?*
   ✓ *Are there any changes needed to be made in your current living situation?*
A. TOTAL *monthly earning needed to cover Living situation:*

_____

_____

Food
✓ *What are you currently spending per month on food?*
   ✓ *Are there changes needed to be made in the amount of money you are spending on food?*
B. TOTAL *monthly earning needed to cover Food:*

_____

_____

Clothes
✓ *What are you currently spending per month on clothes?*
   ✓ *Are there changes needed to be made in the amount of money you are spending on clothes?*
C. TOTAL *monthly earning needed to cover Clothes:*

_____

_____

Health and Wellness
✓ *What are you currently spending per month on activity associated with health (nonfood related)?*

✓ *Are there changes needed to be made in the amount of money you are spending on health and wellness?*

D. TOTAL *monthly earning needed to cover* **Health and Wellness:**

_____

Personal Development

✓ *What are you currently spending per month on activity associated with personal development?*

    ✓ *Are there changes needed to be made in the amount of money you are spending on personal development?*

E. TOTAL *monthly earning needed to cover* **Personal Development:**

_____

Transportation / Auto

✓ *What is your current spending per month on your automobile/transportation?*

    ✓ *Are there any changes needed to be made in your transportation costs?*

F. TOTAL *monthly earning needed to cover* **Transportation:**

_____

Generosity

✓ *What are you currently giving to those in need per month?*

    ✓ *Are there changes needed to be made in the amount of money you are giving?*

G. TOTAL *monthly earning needed to cover* **Generosity:**

_____

Saving

✓ *What are you currently saving per month?*

  ✓ *Are there changes needed to be made in the amount of money you are saving?*

H. **TOTAL** *monthly earning needed to cover Savings:*

Miscellaneous Costs

✓ *What are any miscellaneous costs not listed above?*

  ✓ *Are there changes needed to be made in the amount of money you are spending on any of these costs?*

I. **TOTAL** *monthly earning needed to cover Miscellaneous Costs:*

Rest / Vacation

✓ *What are you currently spending per month on activities that truly refuel you?*

  ✓ *Are there changes needed to be made in the amount of money you are spending on rest?*

J. **TOTAL** *monthly earning needed to cover Rest / Vacation:*

Habits / Pleasures

✓ *What are you currently spending per month on habits or leisure activities?*

  ✓ *Are there changes needed to be made in the amount of money you are spending on leisure?*

K. **TOTAL** *monthly earning needed to cover Leisure Habits:*

THE PURPOSE PARTNER WORKBOOK

1. *How much do you need to make per month to cover all of your expenses (SUM of A-K)?*

Financial Analysis of Wants
What are some healthy wants that you will need to plan for financially?

To be achieved in two years:

_____

_____

_____

_____

_____

_____

2. *How much do you need to be saving today to afford these wants in two years?*

_____

_____

_____

_____

_____

_____

To be achieved in five years:

_____

_____

_____

_____

_____

_____

THE RENEWAL JOURNEY RETREAT

3. How much do you need to be saving today to afford these wants in five years?

_____

_____

_____

_____

_____

_____

_____

Monthly Income Goal (SUM of 1-3):

_____

_____

_____

_____

_____

_____

THE PURPOSE PARTNER WORKBOOK

DAY 6 – RELATIONAL IMPACT

DAY SIX
Relational Impact

Relational abundance requires investment.

Who do you want to see live joy-filled lives?

_____
_____
_____
_____
_____
_____

How can you impact them with the right quantity of quality time?

_____
_____
_____
_____
_____
_____

Is there anyone you need to communicate with about what you are discovering amidst your exploration of needs and wants?

_____
_____
_____
_____
_____
_____

THE PURPOSE PARTNER WORKBOOK

List a few boundaries you need in your career to ensure you have Relational ROI.

1. _____

_____

_____

_____

_____

_____

2. _____

_____

_____

_____

_____

_____

3. _____

_____

_____

_____

_____

_____

4. _____

_____

_____

_____

_____

_____

THE RENEWAL JOURNEY RETREAT

5. _____
_____
_____
_____
_____
_____

THE PURPOSE PARTNER WORKBOOK

DAY 7 - MOTIVATIONAL BOUNDARIES

DAY SEVEN
Understanding Motivational Boundaries

Determining what motivates you and what tempts you will bring forth the right boundaries to live a joy-filled, purposeful life!

What did success look like to your father?

_____
_____
_____
_____
_____
_____
_____

Is his view of success relevant to your view of success?

_____
_____
_____
_____
_____
_____
_____
_____
_____

What did success look like to your mother?

_____
_____
_____
_____
_____
_____
_____

THE PURPOSE PARTNER WORKBOOK

Is her view of success relevant to your view of success?

_____

_____

_____

_____

_____

_____

_____

_____

As you look back at your family of origin are there any expectations of success that you are trying to meet?

_____

_____

_____

_____

_____

_____

_____

_____

Could any pleasures be motivating you toward career ambitions not aligned with your unique purpose?

_____

_____

_____

_____

_____

_____

_____

THE RENEWAL JOURNEY RETREAT

Is trying to impress some person or group keeping you from your true purpose?

_____

_____

_____

_____

_____

_____

_____

What motivates you to be who you want to be?

_____

_____

_____

_____

_____

_____

What top three temptations do you need to be aware of to ensure you are motivated by the right priorities in your life?

1. _____

_____

2. _____

_____

3. _____

_____

_____

THE PURPOSE PARTNER WORKBOOK

DAY 8 - SPIRITUAL NEEDS

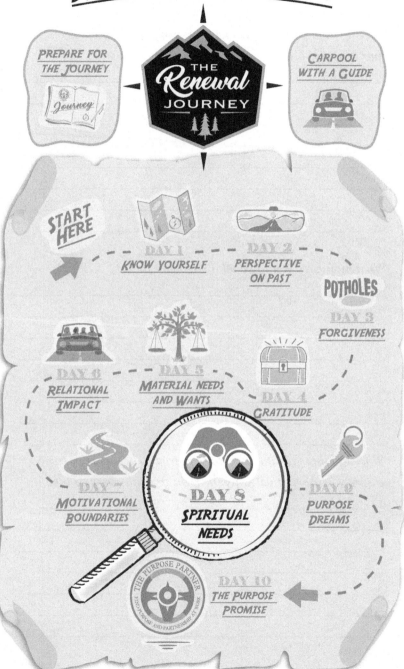

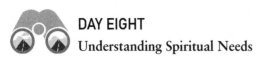

DAY EIGHT
Understanding Spiritual Needs

YOU are uniquely created, loved and designed on purpose for a purpose!

Do you believe that God loves you?

___

What will your loved ones remember you for?

___

What legacy will you leave behind for those you love?

___

THE PURPOSE PARTNER WORKBOOK

Do you see God as the provider of your Material, Relational and Motivational riches?

_____

_____

_____

_____

_____

_____

During the higher times of your life, how were you being provided for?
Materially:

_____

_____

_____

Relationally:

_____

_____

_____

Motivationally:

_____

_____

_____

Spiritually:

_____

_____

_____

During the lower times of your life, how were you being provided for?
Materially:

_____

_____

_____

Relationally:

_____

_____

_____

Motivationally:

_____

_____

_____

Spiritually:

_____

_____

_____

List a few boundaries you need in your career to ensure you can continue to explore your Spiritual Needs

1. _____

_____

_____

_____

_____

THE PURPOSE PARTNER WORKBOOK

2. _____

_____

_____

_____

_____

3. _____

_____

_____

_____

_____

Day Nine
Your Purpose Dreams

PURPOSE DREAMS ANALYSIS

Sweet Spot Analysis

GIFTS
TOP FIVE Passions, Talents and Skills
1. _____
2. _____
3. _____
4. _____
5. _____

MATERIAL NEEDS/WANTS
Monthly Income Goal
_____

Other Total Compensation Needs
_____
_____
_____

RELATIONAL BOUNDARIES
1. _____
2. _____
3. _____
4. _____
5. _____

Motivational Reminder
Specific temptations to be aware of:
1. _____
2. _____
3. _____

Priority Buckets

MUSTS
1. _____
2. _____
3. _____
4. _____
5. _____
6. _____

SHOULDS
1. _____
2. _____
3. _____
4. _____
5. _____
6. _____

NO WAYS
1. _____
2. _____
3. _____
4. _____
5. _____
6. _____

Your Development Plan
Where you want to be in:

1 Year _____
3 Years _____
5 Years _____

THE PURPOSE PARTNER WORKBOOK

DAY 9 - PURPOSE DREAMS

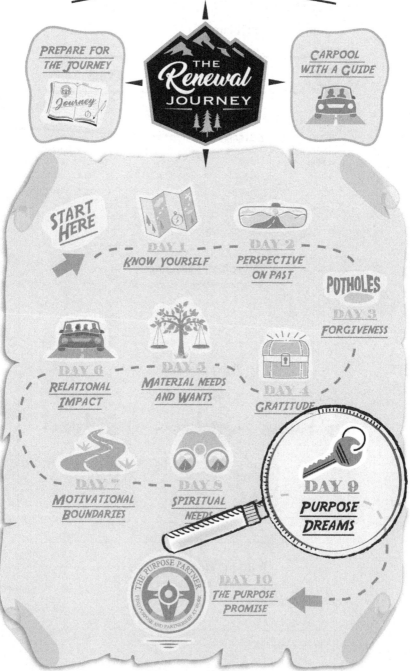

THE RENEWAL JOURNEY RETREAT

*DREAM Big! YOU have what you need to
Partner for Purpose. Let's put it all together!*

Passions: What are the top five things you love to do?

1. _____

_____

_____

_____

2. _____

_____

_____

_____

3. _____

_____

_____

_____

4. _____

_____

_____

_____

5. _____

_____

_____

_____

THE PURPOSE PARTNER WORKBOOK

Talents: What are the top five things you are naturally good at?

1. _____

_____

_____

_____

2. _____

_____

_____

_____

3. _____

_____

_____

_____

4. _____

_____

_____

_____

5. _____

_____

_____

_____

THE RENEWAL JOURNEY RETREAT

Skills: What are the top five things you have learned to be good at?

1. _____

_____

_____

_____

2. _____

_____

_____

_____

3. _____

_____

_____

_____

4. _____

_____

_____

_____

5. _____

_____

_____

_____

THE PURPOSE PARTNER WORKBOOK

Look at your top five passions, talents, and skills. Find the overlap between things you love to do and things you are good at. Distill these to discover your top five gifts.

1. _____
_____
_____
_____

2. _____
_____
_____
_____

3. _____
_____
_____
_____

4. _____
_____
_____
_____

5. _____
_____
_____
_____

Record them now under the heading Gifts in the Sweet Spot Analysis section of your Purpose Dream Analysis.

Your Material Needs and Wants

Record your Monthly Income Goal (Refer to Page 33 in your Workbook)

Record your total compensation needs (Benefits, retirement, and incentives)

1. _____
_____
_____
_____

2. _____
_____
_____
_____

3. _____
_____
_____
_____

Record them now under the Material Needs and Wants section of your Purpose Dream Analysis.

Your Relational Boundaries

List a few boundaries you need in your career to ensure you have Relational ROI. "(Refer to Page 36–37 in your Workbook)

1. _____

2. _____

3. _____

4. _____

5. _____

Record them now under the Relational Boundaries section of your Purpose Dream Analysis.

Your Motivational Reminders

List a few boundaries you need in your career to ensure you are rightly motivated as opposed to falling prey to temptations (Refer to Page 41 in your Workbook)"

1. _____

_____

_____

_____

2. _____

_____

_____

_____

3. _____

_____

_____

_____

4. _____

_____

_____

_____

5. _____

_____

_____

_____

Record them now under the Motivational Reminders section of your Purpose Dream Analysis.

Your Priority Buckets

Your Priority Buckets are the key to unlocking the Purposed Partnerships. Let's start with your MUSTS.

1. *Monthly Income / Compensation Needs* _____

_____

_____

_____

2. _____

_____

_____

_____

3. _____

_____

_____

_____

4. _____

_____

_____

_____

5. _____

_____

_____

_____

Record them now under the MUSTS section of your Purpose Dream Analysis.

THE RENEWAL JOURNEY RETREAT

SHOULDS

List the SHOULD haves to have a Purposed Partnership.

1. _____

_____

_____

_____

2. _____

_____

_____

_____

3. _____

_____

_____

_____

4. _____

_____

_____

_____

5. _____

_____

_____

_____

Record them now under the SHOULDS section of your Purpose Dream Analysis.

NO WAYS

List the NO WAYS to have a Purposed Partnership.

1. _____

2. _____

3. _____

4. _____

5. _____

Record them now under the NO WAYS section of your Purpose Dream Analysis.

Development Plan

What are some personal hopes that you are dreaming about for your future?

_____

_____

What are some family hopes that you are dreaming about for your future?

_____

_____

What are some career development hopes that you are dreaming about for your future?

_____

_____

Summarize your desired development goals using these questions:
In 1 year, I would like to be:

_____

_____

Making:

_____

_____

Developed in these new skill areas:

_____

_____

In 3 years, I would like to be:

_____

_____

Making:

_____

_____

Developed in these new skill areas:

_____

_____

In 5 years, I would like to be:

_____

_____

Making:

_____

_____

Developed in these new skill areas:

_____

_____

*Your completed PDA is the key to starting
a conversation with your employer, your Purposed
Partners. We will support you in that conversation so you
can DREAM BIG to achieve your purpose!*

DAY TEN
The Purpose Promise

Renewal of the mind is a lifestyle. To sustain desirable lifestyles, you must develop the right, purposeful habits.

The Inside-Out life
What are ways you can live an inside-out life?

_____
_____
_____
_____

Live Intentionally
What routines (DO) will help you reach the Purpose Dreams you have found amidst your retreat (BE) time:

Hourly

_____
_____

Daily

_____
_____

Monthly

_____
_____

THE PURPOSE PARTNER WORKBOOK

Quarterly

Yearly

Receive
What habits will help you freely receive?

Embrace Hardship
What habits will help you embrace hardships?

Reduce Noise
What habits will help you reduce noise?

The Next Journey

A Sustained Purposed Partnership

IT HAS BEEN AN HONOR TO BE YOUR GUIDE throughout this journey, but we are not done. We have found what it takes to have a Purposed Partnership. You now know how you best Relate to the most important aspects of who YOU are. You know how these areas can integrate into your work so you can live in your Purpose. And you are Motivated to partner with your employer to find the win/win so you both can be living to embrace your highest RPMs.

The change is exciting for both parties, but a commitment for the long haul is the goal. Your RPMs may change. Your employer wants to see you remain aware of what your true purpose is so they can partner with you.

So, one more Promise that your Partner wants to make you!

Sporadically, your Purpose Guide will connect with you to facilitate a quick check-in. Amidst this check-in, your Purpose Guide will see what has changed in your life and how that may impact your RPMs, your PDA, and your Purposed Partnership. We will then support you as you connect with your employer to re-center to analyze how the partnership is doing.

Your employer is taking a progressive route to show you how important you are to them. They want you to grade them. They are ready to partner with you. They want you to be thriving in all

Relationships, living Purposefully and Motivated to work with them. They are not just talking the talk; they are ready to walk the walk... and they want to walk with you.

Purpose is Found in Partnership

You have the right perspective of YOU. You have your newfound Purpose Dreams. You have a renewed mind and the strength that comes from the joy it produces. And on this tenth day, you have explored habits to sustain purpose. You are equipped for the battle to live with purpose, but you can't do it alone.

On this journey, you were able to refuel what drives you and gain consciousness about how to purposefully integrate your life with your work. Now it is time to develop habits to live in that purpose. It's a HUGE task and we have one encouragement:

DON'T ATTEMPT TO DO IT ALONE!

Your relationships are the critical foundation of living your purpose. It takes a village to sustain a purposeful life and career. You have your employer, your Purposed Partner, to help you remain in your Purpose at work, but you will need to boost your intentionality in all your relationships to sustain the "retreat high" you are feeling right now.

We have walked with thousands of people seeking to live their best life integrated with their work. We have seen people thrive once they define their purpose and we have also seen people struggle to maintain. The common denominator with those who sustain the newfound awareness of their Purpose Dreams is community.

Join us in the movement of purposeful change agents. We're constantly putting new materials out to help you remain within the boundaries of your purpose. You can find those resources at www.purposepromise.org.

A SUSTAINED PURPOSED PARTNERSHIP

Together, we can fuel a purpose-filled movement, and when we do, the world will change. You are part of the solution.

It's time to cultivate purpose together. Work was designed to be a partnership. Life was designed to be a partnership, too. It starts with you intentionally living with purpose, and then your life will be the model for others who you love.

Your destination on The Renewal Journey brought you to a Purposed Partnership at work, and now you are the spark to ignite the journey for others. Pick up others along your road trip for purpose.

The world's standards of success hold power over millions of people. You are no longer conforming to those standards. You are transformed by the Renewal of your mind.

YOU are a vehicle for change!
Let's change the world's drive together!

Work Can Be One of the Greatest Parts of our Life!

Our Mission is to help unfulfilled workers change their view of work and to guide them in the journey to find their unique purpose.

If this mission inspires you, Partner with us to grow the Purpose Movement.

By passing along the resources we have developed to help people find purpose, you are a spark in the Movement. You can find those resources at www.purposepromise.org

If you know of other caring employers ready to Partner for Purpose, please let them know about our process. We can help them achieve their RPMs as their employee Partners find theirs.

Thanks for Partnering with us to reach an amazing destination: A world where each person is aware of how they are uniquely made and can integrate their best life with their work!

Help others find purpose
and purposeful employment
Purposepromise.org

Help other employers embrace
a Purpose Partnership
Purposepartner.org

Listen in and join others
who are living purposefully
Purposepromise.org/podcast